GOD'S CREATIVE POWER®

WILL WORK FOR YOU

by Charles Capps

W9-DAP-055

Updated version contains minor revisions to text, the addition of a Foreword and the scriptures are updated to the New King James Version (NKJV) except as noted.

Unless otherwise indicated, all Scripture quotations are taken from the New King James Version of the Bible.

Scripture quotations marked (LEB) are from the Lexham English Bible. Copyright © 2012 Logos Bible Software. Lexham is a registered trademark of Logos Bible Software.

18   17   16   85   84   83

God's Creative Power® Will Work For You
ISBN-13: 978-0-9820320-6-0
Formerly ISBN-13: 978-0-89274-024-6
Formerly ISBN-10: 0-89274-024-8

Published by Capps Publishing
P. O. Box 69 England, AR 72046

Gods Creative Power® is a registered trademark.

FOREWORD

My father's life was completely turned around by the concepts he shares in this book. I know, because I was a witness. I saw him desperately struggle to stay afloat financially when a "business deal gone bad" left him with a mountain of debt. I witnessed his health failing as he worried himself sick with the stress. The negativity that permeated our house affected me and our entire family as he began to believe he was defeated. Once a successful farmer of cotton, soybeans and rice, his crops began to fail and farming became unproductive where it had once prospered.

I was also present on the day two strangers gave him a little book that changed our family forever. As he read that what you believe and what you speak determines your outcome, he began to study the Word of God to see if it was really true. What he found in the scriptures led him to start speaking the promises of God out loud and personalize them. He called this faith and "confession". Not confession of sin as it is typically assumed, but confession of who you are in Christ and what He has done.

As he spoke to the debt to be paid and disappear, I saw amazing things happen and the debt diminished. His body responded as he spoke healing to it. It rained on his crops and they grew and produced even in drought. He began to share these truths and other peoples' lives were also changed.

Eventually he quit farming and spent the rest of his life teaching the "good news". The God's Creative Power® books have conservatively sold over 6 million copies to date. Much of this is due to thousands of you who buy them by the hundreds to give to others. Like the two strangers who gave that little book to Charles Capps and changed his life, you are giving a book that can change someone forever.

The principles in this book are based on the power of God's Word to transform your life as you declare and speak it into your heart. The transformation of Charles Capps life was a progression over time as yours will be. Be encouraged; things DO change when you apply the Word to your life.

God's Best Be Yours,

Annette Capps

Annette Capps

Chapter 1

GOD'S CREATIVE POWER®
WILL WORK FOR YOU

The Great Confession

Christianity is called the *great confession*, but most Christians who are defeated in life are defeated because they believe and confess the wrong things. They have spoken the words of the enemy, and those *words* hold them in bondage. Proverbs 6:2 says, "...You are snared by the words of your mouth; You are taken by the words of your mouth."

Faith filled words will put you over.

Fear filled words will defeat you.

Words are the most powerful thing in the universe.

Man is a spirit being, very capable of operating on the same level of faith as God.

1

We read in Mark 9:23, "Jesus said to him, 'If you can believe, all things are possible to him who believes.'" Matthew 17:20 says, "So Jesus said to them, 'Because of your unbelief; for assuredly, I say to you, if you have faith as a mustard seed, you will say to this mountain, 'Move from here to there,' and it will move; and nothing will be impossible for you.'" Mark 11:23 says, "For assuredly, I say to you, whoever says to this mountain, 'Be removed and be cast into the sea,' and does not doubt in his heart, but believes that those things he says will be done, he will have whatever he says."

Spiritual Law

This is not theory. It is fact. **It is spiritual law.** It works every time it is applied correctly. This **IS A SPIRITUAL LAW.** *God never does anything without saying it first. God is a faith God. God released His faith in Words.* "So Jesus answered and said to them 'Have faith in God'" (Mark 11:22). A more literal translation of the above verse says, "Have the God kind of faith, or faith of God."

Ephesians 5:1 literally tells us to be imitators of God as children imitate their parents.

To imitate God, you must talk like Him and act like Him.

He would not ask you to do something you are not capable of doing.

Jesus operated in the faith principles of Mark 11:23, and Matthew 17:20 while He was on earth. *He spoke to the wind and sea. He spoke to demons. He spoke to the fig tree. He even spoke to dead men.*

The wind, sea, tree, demons, and even the dead were obedient to what He said.

He operated in the God kind of faith.

*God is a **faith** God. God released **His faith in Words.***

Jesus was imitating His Father and getting the same results as His Father.

In John 14:12 Jesus said, "*...he who believes in Me, the works that I do he will do also; and greater....*"

These principles of faith are based on spiritual laws.

They work for whoever will apply these laws.

You set them in motion by the words of your mouth.

Do you really want all the negative things you have been confessing to come to pass? Are you believing for those things?

If Jesus came to you personally and said, from this day forward it will come to pass, that everything you say will happen exactly as you say it; would that change your vocabulary?

I believe it would.

Binding and Loosing

In Matthew 16:19 Jesus said, "And I will give you the keys of the kingdom of heaven, and whatever you bind on earth will be bound in heaven, and whatever you loose on earth will be loosed in heaven."

Psalms 119:89 tells us, "Forever, O Lord, Your word is settled in heaven." What God said is already established.

Now, it is up to you.

What are you going to say about it?

God will not alter what He has said. "My covenant I will not break, Nor alter the word that has gone out of My lips" (Psalms 89:34).

Whose words will you establish on earth?

The power of binding and loosing is on earth.

Spoken Words

Spoken words program your spirit (heart) either to success or defeat.

Words are containers. They carry faith, or fear, and they produce after their kind.

"So then faith comes by hearing, and hearing by the Word of God" (Romans 10:17). Faith comes more quickly when you hear yourself quoting, speaking, and saying the things God said. You will more readily receive God's Word into your spirit by hearing yourself say it than if you hear someone else say it.

Live in the Authority of the Word

The Spirit of God spoke to me concerning confessing the Word of God out loud: where you can hear yourself saying it.

He said, "It is a scientific application of the wisdom of God to the psychological makeup of man."

And it works, thank God. *The body of Christ must begin to live in the authority of the Word. For God's Word is creative power.* That Creative power is produced by the heart, formed by the tongue, and released out of the mouth in word form.

In August of 1973, The Word of the Lord came unto me saying, "If men would believe me, long prayers are not necessary. Just speaking the Word will bring what you desire. My creative power is given to man in Word form. I have ceased for a time from my work and have given man the book of MY CREATIVE POWER. That power is STILL IN MY WORD.

"For it to be effective, man must speak it in faith. Jesus spoke it when He was on earth and as it worked then so shall it work now. *But it must be spoken by the body.* Man must rise up and have dominion over the power of evil by my Words. It is my greatest desire that my people create a better life by the spoken Word. For my Word has not lost its power just because it has been spoken once. It is still equally as powerful today as when I said, 'Let there be light.'

"But for my Word to be effective, **men must speak it**, and that creative power will come forth performing that which is spoken in faith.

"My Word is not void of power.

"My people are void of speech. They hear the world and speak as the world speaks. By observing circumstances they have lost sight of my Word. They even speak that which the enemy says, and they destroy their own inheritance by corrupt communication of fear and unbelief.

"No Word of Mine is void of power, only powerless when it is unspoken.

7

"As there is creative power in my Spoken Word, so is there evil power present in the words of the enemy to affect and oppress everyone that speaks them.

"Be not conformed, but be transformed into the body of faith, knowing that my Words are alive evermore. Believe, speak, and obtain that your joy may be full and you shall be complete in Me."

These truths changed my life. I have never been the same.

Confess victory in the face of apparent defeat. Confess abundance in the face of apparent lack.

In June of 1974, I was teaching a faith seminar in Hickory, North Carolina. My text was taken from Mark 11:23. The Word of the Lord came to me as I was teaching and spoke one of the most profound statements I have ever heard. It was simple, but then Jesus never made anything hard to understand. It is so simple that it almost seems foolish, but it has changed many lives.

It will change yours as you receive it.

Let's put it in the context of which He spoke. Mark 11:23, "For assuredly, I say to you, whoever says to this mountain, 'Be removed and be cast into the sea,' and does not doubt in his heart, but believes that those things he says will be done, he will have whatever he says."

As I was teaching from this text, Jesus said to me, "*I have told my people they can have WHAT THEY SAY, but they are SAYING WHAT THEY HAVE.*"

That is a very simple truth, but oh how profound and far reaching. For as long as you say what you have, you will have what you say, then you, again say what you have, and it will produce no more than what you say.

You can see that you have set a spiritual law in motion that will confine you to the very position or circumstance you are in when you set that law in motion. It is an age old problem of not looking beyond what you can see with the physical eye.

A correct application of this spiritual law will change even the most impossible situation. But, to incorrectly apply these laws will hold you in bondage and cause the circumstance to grow worse.

Every faith principle, every spiritual law that God set forth in His Word was for your benefit. *It was designed to put you over in life.*

Learn to Release Your Faith in Words

You can have what you say if you learn to release faith from the heart in your words.

Jesus said, "...as you have believed, it will be done for you." (Matthew 8:13 LEB). *He didn't say it would only work if you believed right. Whether you believe right, or wrong, it is still the law.* "...God is not mocked, for whatever a man sows, that he will also reap" (Galatians 6:7).

The spiritual law is based on the same basic principle of seed-time harvest. The words you speak are seeds that produce after their kind. Just as sure as they are planted, you can be equally sure a harvest will follow.

Faith talks. When faith talks, it talks faith, not fear and unbelief.

The Treasures of the Heart cannot be Hidden, but are Manifest Through Words

Learn to take the Words of Jesus personally.

In Mark 11:23, Jesus tells you that you can have what you say if what you say comes from faith in your heart.

What would happen if Jesus walked down the aisles of your church, laid His hands on the people, and said, "It will come to pass that after I have laid my hand on each one of you, everything you say will happen just as you say it?"

Half of the congregation would jump up and say, "That just *tickles me to death!*"

The enemy has so programmed the minds of people until instead of resisting him, they have just sort of buddied up with him, and begun to talk his language.

Train Yourself to Speak God's Word

Let us train ourselves to speak God's Word. Ephesians 5:1 tells us, "Therefore be imitators of God, as dear children." *We are to imitate God as a child does his father.* If a child imitates his father, he will walk like him, talk like him, and pattern his every move after him.

We should do no less after our Father, God.

When you study the life of Jesus you find several important facts that caused Him to overcome the world, the flesh, and the devil. I will list a few.

1. He spent much time in prayer, but He never prayed the problem, He prayed the answer — **what God said is the answer.**

2. He spoke accurately, never crooked speech. His conversation always consisted of what God said.

3. He always spoke the end results, **not the problem**. Never — did He confess **present** circumstances. He spoke the **desired results**.

4. He used the written Word to defeat Satan.

THE WORD OF GOD CONCEIVED IN THE HEART, FORMED BY THE TONGUE, AND SPOKEN OUT OF THE MOUTH IS CREATIVE POWER.

Chapter 2

GOD'S WORD IS MEDICINE

Proverbs 4:20-22, *"...give attention to my words... for they are life...and health (medicine) to all their flesh."*

God's Word ministers to the total man. His Word (Jesus) is our wisdom, righteousness, sanctification and redemption.

Most people have used the words of their mouth to hold themselves in bondage. But as you begin to speak the Word of God from the heart, it will produce liberty. It will produce the health and healing the Word said it would.

Most people have spoken contrary to the Word. They have spoken things that the devil has said. They have quoted what the enemy has said about them. Therefore, they have established on earth the words the enemy has said.

If we will begin to **establish the things God said**, and **establish His Word on this earth**, then thank God! We'll rise to a new *level of faith*.

We will **walk in the level of life where we release the ability of God** *by the words of our mouth*. We can release the ability of God within ourselves by the words of our mouth and cause **His Word** and **His power** to become **available to us**.

Let's learn to take God's medicine daily.

God's ℞

*no harmful side effects.

To Defeat Worry and Fear
Confess These Three Times a Day

I am the body of Christ and Satan has no power over me. For I overcome evil with good (1 Corinthians 12:27; Romans 12:21).

---

*These are not direct quotations from the Bible but these are paraphrased confessions based on the Scriptures under them.

I am of God and have overcome him (Satan). For greater is He that is in me, than he that is in the world (1 John 4:4).

***

I will fear no evil for you are with me Lord, your Word and your Spirit they comfort me (Psalms 23:4).

***

I am far from oppression, and fear does not come near me (Isaiah 54:14).

***

No weapon formed against me shall prosper, for my righteousness is of the Lord. But whatever I do will prosper for I'm like a tree that's planted by the rivers of water (Isaiah 54:17; Psalms 1:3).

***

I am delivered from the evils of this present world for it is the will of God. (Galatians 1:4).

***

No evil will befall me neither shall any plague come near my dwelling. For the Lord has given His angels charge over me and they keep me in all my ways, and in my pathway is life and there is no death (Psalms 91:10-11; Proverbs 12:28).

***

I am a doer of the Word of God and am blessed in my deeds. I am happy in those things which I do because I am a doer of the Word of God (James 1:22).

I take the shield of faith and I quench every fiery dart that the wicked one brings against me (Ephesians 6:16).

***

Christ has redeemed me from the curse of the law. Therefore, I forbid any sickness or disease to come upon this body. Every disease germ and every virus that touches this body dies instantly in the name of Jesus. Every organ and every tissue of this body functions in the perfection to which God created it to function, and I forbid any malfunction in this body, in the name of Jesus (Galatians 3:13; Romans 8:11; Genesis 1:31; Matthew 16:19).

***

I am an overcomer and I overcome by the blood of the Lamb and the word of my testimony (Revelation 12:11).

***

I am submitted to God and the devil flees from me because I resist him in the name of Jesus (James 4:7).

***

The Word of God is forever settled in heaven. Therefore, I establish His Word upon this earth" (Psalms 119:89).

***

Great is the peace of my children for they are taught of the Lord (Isaiah 54:13).

***

If Overweight, Take This Capps'-sule Before Meals Three Times A Day

I don't desire to eat so much I become overweight. I present my body to God, my body is the temple of the Holy Ghost, who dwells in me. I am not my own, I am bought with a price therefore, in the name of Jesus I refuse to over-eat. Body settle down, in the name of Jesus and conform to the Word of God. I mortify the desires of this body and command it to come into line with the Word of God (Romans 12:1; 1 Corinthians 6:19).

***

For Material Needs Confess These Three Times a Day Until They're Manifest

Christ has redeemed me from the curse of the law. Christ has redeemed me from poverty, Christ has redeemed me from sickness, Christ has redeemed me from spiritual death (Galatians 3:13; Deuteronomy 28).

***

For poverty He has given me wealth, for sickness He has given me health, for death He has given me eternal life (2 Corinthians 8:9; Isaiah 53:5-6; John 10:10; John 5:24).

***

It is true unto me according to the Word of God (Psalms 119:25).

***

I delight myself in the Lord and He gives me the desires of my heart (Psalms 37:4).

***

I have given and it is given to me good measure, pressed down, shaken together and running over (Luke 6:38).

***

With what measure I use, it is measured back to me. I sow bountifully, therefore I reap bountifully. I give cheerfully, and My God has made all grace abound toward me and I have all sufficiency in all things and have an abundance for every good work (2 Corinthians 9:6-8).

***

There is no lack for my God supplies all of my need according to His riches in glory by Christ Jesus (Philippians 4:19).

***

The Lord is my shepherd and I DO NOT WANT. Jesus was made poor, that I through His poverty might have abundance. For He came that I might have life and have it more abundantly (Psalms 23:1; 2 Corinthians 8:9; John 10:10).

***

I, having received abundance of grace and the gift of righteousness do reign as a king in life by Jesus Christ (Romans 5:17).

***

The Lord has pleasure in the prosperity of His servant, and Abraham's blessings are mine (Psalms 35:27; Galatians 3:14).

***

For Wisdom and Guidance Confess These Three Times a Day Until it is Manifest

The Spirit of truth abides in me and teaches me all things, and He guides me into all truths. Therefore I confess I have perfect knowledge of every situation and every circumstance in life. For I have the wisdom of God (John 16:13; James 1:5).

***

I trust in the Lord with all my heart, and I lean not on my own understanding (Proverbs 3:5).

***

In all my ways I acknowledge Him and He directs my path (Proverbs 3:6).

***

The Lord will perfect that which concerns me (Psalms 138:8).

***

I let the Word of Christ dwell in me richly in all wisdom (Colossians 3:16).

***

I do follow the Good Shepherd and I know His voice and the voice of a stranger I will not follow (John 10:4-5).

***

Jesus is made unto me wisdom, righteousness, sanctification, and redemption. Therefore I confess I have the wisdom of God, and I am the righteousness of God in Christ Jesus (1 Corinthians 1:30; 2 Corinthians 5:21).

***

I am filled with the knowledge of the Lord's will in all wisdom and spiritual understanding (Colossians 1:9).

***

I am a new creation in Christ, I am His workmanship created in Christ Jesus. Therefore I have the mind of Christ and the wisdom of God is formed within me (2 Corinthians 5:17; Ephesians 2:10; 1 Corinthians 2:16).

***

I have put off the old man and have put on the new man, which is renewed in the knowledge after the image of Him that created me (Colossians 3:10).

***

I receive the Spirit of wisdom and revelation in the knowledge of God, the eyes of my understanding being enlightened. And I am not conformed to this world but am transformed by the renewing of my mind. My mind is renewed by the Word of God (Ephesians 1:17-18; Romans 12:2).

***

For Comfort and Strength Confess These as Often as Necessary

I am increasing in the knowledge of God. I am strengthened with all might according to His glorious power (Colossians 1:10-11).

***

I am delivered from the power of darkness and I am translated into the kingdom of His dear Son (Colossians 1:13).

***

I am born of God and I have world overcoming faith residing on the inside of me. For greater is He that is in me, than he that is in the world (I John 5:4-5; 1 John 4:4).

***

I will do all things through Christ who strengthens me (Philippians 4:13).

***

The joy of the Lord is my strength. The Lord is the strength of my life (Nehemiah 8:10; Psalms 27:1).

***

The peace of God which passes all understanding keeps my heart and my mind through Christ Jesus. And things which are good, and pure, and perfect, and lovely, and of good report, I think on these things (Philippians 4:7-8).

***

I let no corrupt communication come out of my mouth, but that which is good to edifying, that it may minister grace to the hearer. I grieve not the Holy Spirit of God, who has sealed me unto the day of redemption (Ephesians 4:29).

***

I speak the truth of the Word of God in love and I grow up into the Lord Jesus Christ in all things (Ephesians 4:15).

***

No man shall take me out of His hand for I have eternal life (John 10:28-29).

***

I let the peace of God rule in my heart and I refuse to worry about anything (Colossians 3:15).

***

I will not let the Word of God depart from before my eyes because it is life to me and it is health and healing to all my flesh (Proverbs 4:21-22).

***

God is on my side. God is in me now, who can be against me? He has given unto me all things that pertain unto life and godliness. Therefore I am a partaker of His divine nature (2 Corinthians 6:16; John 10:10; 2 Peter 1:3-4; Romans 8:31).

***

I am a believer and these signs do follow me. In the name of Jesus I cast out demons, I speak with new tongues, I lay hands on the sick and they do recover (Mark 16:17-18).

***

Jesus gave me the authority to use His name. And that which I bind on earth is bound in heaven. And that which I loose on earth is loosed in heaven. Therefore in the name of the Lord Jesus Christ I bind the principalities, the powers, the rulers of the darkness of this world. I bind and cast down spiritual wickedness in high places and render them harmless and ineffective against me in the name of Jesus (Matthew 16:19; John 16:23-24; Ephesians 6:12).

***

I am complete in Him who is the head of all principality and power. For I am His workmanship, created in Christ Jesus for good works which God has ordained that I should walk in them (Colossians 2:10; Ephesians 2:10).

***

God created the universe by the methods which you have just put into motion by the words of your mouth. *God released His faith in words.* Man is created in the image of God, therefore man releases his faith in words. Words are the most powerful things in the universe today.

Let me say it again, "The Word of God conceived in the human spirit, formed by the tongue, and spoken out of the mouth becomes creative power that will work for you.

If the body of Christ would only grasp the truths and the principles that are taught in this book, and put them in action, they could change the world.

Jesus said, "I HAVE TOLD MY PEOPLE THEY CAN HAVE WHAT THEY SAY" but "MY PEOPLE ARE SAYING WHAT THEY HAVE."

NEW RELEASE!!!

Calling Things That Are Not

The Powerful Realm of the Unseen

The principle of calling things that are not as though they were is the spiritual principle through which everything physical becomes manifest. God created light by calling for "light" when only darkness was there. Jesus used this same method, call the lepers clean, and the dead to life, and peace to the storm.

You must call for what you desire. If you want your dog to come, you call the dog. You call for what is not there. Whatever you call in the natural will come. Call what does not exist and continue to call until it manifests.

ISBN 13: 978-1-937578-31-2

Charles Capps a farmer from England, Arkansas became an internationally known Bible teacher by sharing practical truths from the Word of God. His simplistic, down to earth style of applying spiritual  principles to daily life has appealed to people from every Christian denomination.

The requests for speaking engagements became so great after the printing of God's Creative Power® Will Work for You© that he retired from farming and became a full-time Bible teacher. His books are available in multiple languages throughout the world.

Besides publishing 24 books, including best-sellers The Tongue A Creative Force and God's Creative Power® series which has sold over 6 million copies, Capps Ministries has a national daily radio broadcast and weekly TV broadcast called "Concepts of Faith".

For a complete list of CDs, DVDs, and books
by Charles Capps, or to receive his
publication, Concepts of Faith, write:

Charles Capps Ministries

P.O. Box 69, England, Arkansas 72046

Toll Free Order Line (24 hours)

1-877-396-9400

www.charlescapps.com

BOOKS BY CHARLES CAPPS AND ANNETTE CAPPS

Angels

God's Creative Power® for Finances

God's Creative Power® - Gift Edition
(Also available in Spanish)

BOOKS BY ANNETTE CAPPS

Quantum Faith®

*Reverse The Curse in
Your Body and Emotions*

Overcoming Persecution

Powerful Teaching From Charles Capps

If you have enjoyed reading this book, you can find more dynamic teaching from Charles Capps in this revolutionary book.

Triumph Over The Enemy

In Second Corinthians 12:7, Paul writes about "a thorn in the flesh, the messenger of Satan" who had been sent to harass him. This "messenger" was sent to create problems and stir up the people against Paul everywhere he preached. But Paul knew the key to overcoming this obstacle – he learned to exercise his God-given authority here on the earth!

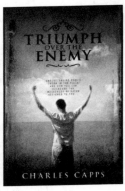

This book will show you how to walk in God's grace and triumph over this enemy sent to harass and keep you from God's greater blessings in your life.

ISBN-13: 978-0-9819574-2-5